INCLUSION
ACTIVITIES THAT WORK!

Toby J.
KARTEN

CORWIN PRESS
Classroom

For information:

Corwin Press
A SAGE Publications Company
2455 Teller Road
Thousand Oaks, California 91320
CorwinPress.com

SAGE Publications, Ltd.
1 Oliver's Yard
55 City Road
London EC1Y 1SP
United Kingdom

SAGE Publications India Pvt. Ltd.
B 1/I 1 Mohan Cooperative
Industrial Area
Mathura Road, New Delhi
India 110 044

SAGE Publications Asia-Pacific Pvt. Ltd.
33 Pekin Street #02-01
Far East Square
Singapore 048763

ISBN 978-1-4129-5235-4

This book is printed on acid-free paper.

08 09 10 11 12 10 9 8 7 6 5 4 3 2 1

Executive Editor: Kathleen Hex
Managing Developmental Editor: Christine Hood
Editorial Assistant: Anne O'Dell
Proofreader: Bette Darwin
Art Director: Anthony D. Paular
Cover Designer: Rose Storey
Cover Production Artist: Karine Hosvepian
Interior Production Artists: Karine Hovsepian and Scott Van Atta

INCLUSION
ACTIVITIES THAT WORK!

GRADES **3–5**

TABLE OF CONTENTS

Connections to Standards

This chart shows the national standards that are covered in each chapter.

LANGUAGE ARTS	Standards are covered on pages
1	12, 22, 23, 24, 25
3	14, 16, 19, 22, 23, 24, 25, 26, 28, 29, 30, 31, 32, 33, 34, 35
4	36, 41, 44, 45, 46, 47
5	36, 41, 44, 45, 46, 47

MATH EMATICS	Standards are covered on pages
Numbers and Operations 1	55
Numbers and Operations 2	49, 52, 55
Numbers and Operations 3	49, 55
Algebra 3	55
Geometry 1	58, 59
Geometry 2	58, 59
Geometry 3	57, 58, 59
Geometry 4	55, 57, 58, 59
Measurement 1	74
Measurement 2	74

SCIENCE	Standards are covered on pages
Physical Science—Understand properties of objects and materials	65
Life Science—Understand characteristics of organisms	74
Life Science—Understand organisms and environments	62, 65
Earth and Space Science—Identify objects in the sky	70
Science and Technology—Ability to distinguish between natural objects and objects made by humans	36
Science and Technology—Understand about science and technology	62
Science in Personal and Social Perspectives—Understand the importance of personal health	65, 74
History and Nature of Science—Understand science as a human endeavor	60, 62, 65

SOCIAL STUDIES	Standards are covered on pages
Understand the interactions among people, places, and environments	64, 65
Understand culture and cultural diversity	81, 82, 83, 84, 85
Understand the ways human beings view themselves in and over time	62, 71, 72, 75, 77, 81, 82, 83, 84, 85
Understand the interactions among people, places, and environments	26, 62, 64, 65, 81, 82, 83, 84, 85
Understand individual development and identity	29, 30, 31, 32, 33, 34, 35, 47, 60, 62, 68, 71, 72, 75, 77, 81, 82, 83, 84, 85
Understand interactions among individuals, groups, and institutions	29, 30, 31, 32, 33, 34, 35, 77, 81, 82, 84, 85
Understand global connections and interdependence	64, 65

Introduction

Educators teaching students with exceptionalities in general education classrooms need practical tools and strategies to help ease their workloads, while meeting individual needs and standards at the same time. As difficult as it may sound, it is indeed possible to simultaneously embrace standards and differences, differences in abilities, learning styles, and intelligences. With the right tools, appropriate accommodations and modifications can be seamlessly and appropriately applied.

This book attempts to ease frustrations and replace them with proactive, research-based, effective strategies that apply across the curriculum. A multitude of activities offer practical ways to embrace educational standards, while differentiating the learning. These activities are not intended to replace your curriculum. Instead, they are designed to enhance your instructional repertoire through active learning environments that accommodate students' differing needs.

As an educator, you know your students best. The activities in this book can be adapted or modified to meet the needs of specific students in your classroom. In addition, this book includes teacher-friendly inclusion forms designed to simplify the inclusion process. Use them to help with documentation, communication, reflection, organization, and inclusion implementation. These forms help break through the educational jargon to provide direct, simple support.

As educators, meeting the standards is not the goal; *exceeding* the standards is the goal! Instead of thinking "My students can't do this," change your thought process to "*How* can I get them to do this?" Concentrate on strengths, not weaknesses. The eighteen activities on page 7 are the backbone of the lessons offered in this book. These approaches can be applied to a student with vision or hearing impairment, a student who has high cognitive needs, a student with behavioral challenges, as well as a student with more advanced skills. This book provides the "roadmap" to inspire the potentials and strengths of all learners and educators. Enjoy the journey!

Valuable Everyday Activities to Promote Inclusion

- Establish prior knowledge.

- Preplan lessons with structured objectives, allowing for inter- and post-planning.

- Proceed from the simple to the complex by using discrete task analysis, which breaks up learning into its parts, while still valuing the whole.

- Use a step-by-step approach, teaching in small bites, with lots of practice and repetition for those who need it.

- Reinforce abstract concepts with concrete examples.

- Think about possible accommodations and modifications that might be needed.

- Incorporate sensory elements including visual, auditory, and kinesthetic/tactile.

- Teach to students' strengths to help compensate for their weaknesses.

- Concentrate on individual students, not syndromes.

- Provide opportunities for success to build self-esteem.

- Give positives before negatives.

- Use modeling with both teachers and peers.

- Vary types of instruction and assessment, with multiple intelligences and cooperative learning.

- Make learning relevant by relating it to students' lives using interest inventories.

- Remember the basics, proper hygiene, respecting others, and effective listening, in addition to the "three R's": reading, writing, and arithmetic.

- Establish a pleasant classroom environment that encourages students to ask questions and become actively involved in their learning.

- Increase students' self-awareness of levels and progress.

- Provide many opportunities to effectively communicate and collaborate with parents, students, and colleagues.

Put It into Practice

Special education is at a crossroads—crossroads that have been repaved and redirected again and again. Why can't we just get it right? The answer is that perhaps there is no "universal right." We strive for universal rights in our world, yet differing political, economic, social, spiritual, and in this case, educational thoughts and policies abound. Academia conducts research, studies are carried out, and theories about best practices are born. The ultimate goal is to transfer the research into immediate practical benefits for students in that laboratory called the classroom.

The dilemma is that we live in a diverse world, one in which people have differing needs and abilities. Consequently, how could these theories then be universal? Is there such a thing as a universal lesson that meets the needs of all students? Can a student with severe cognitive impairments benefit from the same strategies as a student with more advanced skills? It is a challenge we all face in today's inclusive classrooms.

Instructional strategies are only beneficial when they match students' diverse needs. Administrators, educators, parents, and even students can become frustrated by the ever-changing legislative demands that although designed to benefit those with special needs, often create schisms among personnel at school, caregivers at home, and students themselves. Professionals need to both apply and raise curriculum standards making sure everyone is on the same page. The purpose here is to erase frustrations and replace them with research-based, effective strategies that apply across the curriculum, and that embrace school and home environments, and the potentials and strengths of all learners (Odom, Brantlinger, Gersten, Horner, Thompson, & Harris, 2005).

For example, students who have phonemic awareness skills are likely to have an easier time learning to read and spell than students who have few or none of these skills (Armbruster & Osborn, 2001). The National Council for Teacher of Mathematics says that students in grades K–2 must have standards that help them understand numbers, ways of representing numbers, relationships among numbers, and number systems. Do these standards apply for all or just some learners? Now that inclusion is the thrust, educators are compelled and driven to find ways to deliver the same standards to students of differing abilities. This needs to begin at these crucial early grades.

Educators can effectively instruct students of all abilities and potentials, having high regard for all, while embracing individuality.

Professionals can design lessons that include students with exceptionalities, such as those with diverse physical, behavioral, social, learning, and cognitive levels. The standards in general education must be accessible to those students with the most and least needs, and everyone in between! Classrooms must create a healthy environment that both recognizes and nurtures students' strengths, so they can flourish into critical thinkers, ready to tackle the many challenges in their academic future.

Students are assessed on the knowledge they gain. Schools are required to meet Adequate Yearly Progress (AYP) under No Child Left Behind (NCLB), with the Individuals with Disabilities Education Act (IDEA) still in place (Yell, Katsiyanna, & Shiner, 2006). Before alternate assessments are given, educators must look at the general education curriculum requirements and then make some decisions.

In the past, many learners with exceptionalities were often deleted from mainstream learning and placed in separate classes with lower requirements (Walsh & Conner, 2004). Unfortunately, this mindset then resulted in an adult population ill prepared to meet societal demands in the workforce and in social relationships. Today, special and general educators must collaborate to figure out ways that all students can and will be successful in school by creating and instilling high expectations, beginning with the early, formative grades.

Effective research studies and literature, with reference to specific instructional strategies, reveal the need for change (Harriott, 2004; Karten, 2005; McTighe, Seif, & Wiggins, 2004; Nolet & McLaughlin, 2005; Zull, 2004). Educators in the field are arduously trying to include students with special needs general education classrooms. In effort, researchers, administrators, parents, students, and teachers can all play on the same team. Delivering knowledge through principles such as step-by-step-learning while accommodating for individual differences and strengths results in strategic, meaningful, applicable, and long-lasting learning for all!

CHAPTER 1

Reading

Teachers sometimes assume that students possess prior knowledge and prerequisite skills in reading and move on to the next topic. If reading skills are shaky, then well-planned lessons become futile. Should all students know every consonant and vowel sound by the time they enter third, fourth, or even fifth grade? Many of them will; but some students, especially those with learning challenges, may have missed one or two crucial steps in earlier grades.

Teaching phonological awareness is not restricted to the early primary grades. It should be continually emphasized and refined in the intermediary grades as well. The English language is far too complex for children to keep pace with all the words they encounter; therefore, a solid foundation is essential to future development. The following activities will reinforce essential reading skills and help to fill in the gaps students may have missed along the way.

Finding Words in Words

This activity challenges students to draw from their spelling and vocabulary skills to make new words. *Please* may seem like a simple word; however, students have the possibility of finding 32 words in this one word. Give each student a copy of the **Stop and Find New Words! reproducible (page 11)**. Invite students to study the word and write as many new words as they can by rearranging the letters. (Tell students not to include any proper names.)

Inclusion Tips

Encourage further letter play by inviting students to play games like Scrabble or Boggle.

Have students create their own word searches or crossword puzzles using Discovery School's Puzzlemaker Web site at www.puzzlemaker.com.

Stop and Find New Words!

Directions: How many words can you find in the word *please*?
Write them on the lines below.

PLEASE

Two letters:

_____   _____

Three letters:

_____   _____   _____

_____   _____   _____

_____   _____   _____

Four letters:

_____   _____   _____

_____   _____   _____

_____   _____   _____

_____   _____

Five letters:

_____   _____   _____

_____   _____   _____

_____

Five Rules for Reading

These five reading rules are simple and direct strategies for helping students approach text. Model these rules for students whenever you can—introduce, model, and practice!

1. Sound out the word by looking at vowel and consonant patterns (for vowels, this means *a, e, i, o, u*, or any combination of these letters at the beginning, middle, or end of words). Vowels can be short, long, r-controlled, or combined with another vowel. Consonants can also be blends (e.g., *fl, sp, pl, st*) or digraphs (e.g., *wh, sh, th, ch*). Digraphs can also combine with other consonants (e.g., *shrimp, lunch*).

2. Try to say one syllable at a time; each syllable needs at least one vowel.

3. Find word parts by looking for root words, prefixes, and suffixes.

4. Use context clues to find the meaning of unknown words by reading the surrounding words in the sentence or paragraph. Understand the sentence in relation to the passage.

5. Find word meaning and pronunciation in a dictionary or on the computer.

Give students a copy of the **Five Rules for Reading reproducible (page 13)**. Review the rules with students, modeling as needed. Then have them fill in their charts.

Inclusion Tips

Students with IEPs are often concerned that they complete the same work as peers. They do not want simpler, or what they perceive to be "watered down," work. This generic reproducible can be assigned to all students yet individualized to support different reading levels with varied book choices.

Reading unfamiliar words should be an ongoing practice across the curriculum to maintain and strengthen word-decoding skills. Break up newly introduced vocabulary words into syllables, no matter what the subject!

Five Rules for Reading!

Directions: Use these five reading rules to help you figure out words whenever you read.

Reading Rules

1. Sound out words by looking at vowel and consonant patterns.
   - Vowels (*a, e, i, o, u*) can have a long or a short sound, be r-controlled, or combine with other vowels to make new sounds (e.g., *ea, ou, oa*).

   - Consonants can stand alone or be part of a blend, two or more letters with separate sounds (e.g., *fl, st, cl, spl*), or a digraph, two letters with one sound (e.g, *wh, sh, th, ch*).

2. Read one syllable at a time (e.g., *dic-tion-ar-y*).

3. Find word parts by looking for root words, prefixes, and suffixes.

4. Use context clues to find the meaning of unknown words. *Context clues* are the words surrounding an unknown word in a sentence or paragraph.

5. Look up words in a dictionary or on a computer. You can find the definition and pronunciation.

Directions: Choose four words from a story you are reading. Write them in the chart. Write which reading rule helped you figure out how to say and understand each word?

Word	Rule Used

Breaking Up Words

Students can use many methods to figure out how to pronounce words, such as breaking up words into syllables, sounds, or word parts. Increasing awareness of how words are formed allows learners to transfer decoding skills to their reading. Large words can be intimidating to students. Breaking up larger words into prefixes, suffixes, and root words allows students to recognize smaller, more readable parts. It also helps them with comprehension as they apply these word parts to other words they read.

Give each student several copies of the **Breaking Up Words reproducible (page 15)**. As students read, individually or as a class, invite them to break down larger words into readable, comprehendible parts. They can keep the chart in a reading folder to use as a reference. You can also make an enlarged classroom chart for whole-group reading.

Inclusion Tip

Students with attention, reading, and other learning issues appreciate this type of external, logical, and structured organization. Although you may be challenged initially, stick with this systematic program. The benefits are enormous!

Prefix	Base/Root	Suffix	Compound Word	Page #
tele	phone			3
			butterfly	7
	though	less		13
	child	hood		18
			homemade	22

Name _____ Date _____

Breaking Up Words

Directions: As you read, write larger words in the chart below. Break up the words into prefixes, suffixes, root words, and compound words. Write the page number where you found the word.

Book Title:_____

Prefix	Base/Root Word	Suffix	Compound Word	Page #

Classifying Words: Nouns, Verbs, Adjectives, Adverbs

This activity invites students to become active readers as they familiarize themselves with the variety of words writers use to describe, entertain, inform, and persuade. Give students a copy of the **Classifying Words reproducible (page 17)**. They will use this chart to classify words by part of speech: nouns, verbs, adjectives, and adverbs. As with other reproducibles in this section, the chart can be used again and again.

As students read literature and other texts, have them categorize and write words of interest in the appropriate columns. This not only reinforces parts of speech, but also helps students develop a running list of interesting words they can use in their own writing!

Inclusion Tip

Students with sight impairment or dyslexia can listen to books on tape and orally complete the same assignment if writing is too demanding. Contact Recording for the Blind and Dyslexic at www.rfbd.org to obtain CDs of digital audio books.

Asking Questions

Some students can read words correctly but have difficulty making meaning from or processing the information they read. If you ask students about a piece of literature, they sometimes have difficulty understanding the question or making meaning from your inquiry. The following activity invites students to think critically about text and develop their own questions.

Give students a copy of the **Asking Questions reproducible (page 18)**. Before they begin, model an example for the class and encourage students to respond with their own questions.

Inclusion Tips

Students with processing disorders or cognitive needs may require a modified assignment that asks them to write just one type of question. For example, they might concentrate on Main Idea or Details before moving on to Inference.

Stock a variety of books with assorted reading and interest levels in your classroom library. Include easier picture books to model and practice comprehension skills.

Name _____ Date _____

Classifying Words

Directions: Just like there are different kinds of music—rap, rock, pop, classical—there are different kinds of words. Nouns, verbs, adjectives, and adverbs make bland sentences much more interesting!

Use this chart to classify words from your reading.

Nouns Nouns name a person, place, thing, or idea.	Verbs Verbs describe action, expression, or occurrence.	Adjectives Adjectives describe a noun or pronoun.	Adverbs Adverbs describe verbs, adjectives, and other adverbs.

Asking Questions

Directions: After reading a story, write a question for each of these reading skills. Then exchange papers with a classmate.

Main Idea: This is the most important idea of the story. Asking about the main idea might involve using words such as **who**, **what**, **when**, **where**, **why**, **or how**. Find the main idea and rewrite it as a question.

Main Idea Question: _____

Details: These are facts that tell more about the main idea. Details may be specific names, dates, examples, or descriptions.

Details Question: _____

Predictions: Predictions deal with the future. Think about what might happen next in the plot or what might happen to the characters.

Prediction Question: _____

Inferences: An inference is looking beyond the written words. It is figuring out what the author hinted at but did not actually say. Inferences must be supported by an example, a comparison, or a connection between events and details.

Inference Question: _____

Sequencing: This is the order of events in a story. Words to find sequence include *first*, *then*, *next*, *later*, *after*, and *finally*. These, along with other story clues, help you find the sequence.

Sequencing Question: _____

Troublesome Words

Over the course of several years, I recorded students' misread words and phrases. Many were phonetic mistakes. Misread phonemes can get in the way of vocabulary development and comprehension. Mistakes should be addressed, identified, and phased out of common practice. This type of "word-a-cognition" (awareness of words) helps students correct their own phonetic mistakes as they develop as readers.

Reproduce the **Word-a-Cognition reproducible (page 20)**, one for each student in your class. Set aside time to listen to and/or record students as they read aloud during everyday literature study or silent reading time. You can comfortably meet with five students in half an hour to complete their Word-a-Cognition sheets. Meet with students individually to go over mistakes and misread words and phrases. Later, you can incorporate students' mistakes into a general class lesson, keeping students' mistakes anonymous. Students might find that they make many of the same mistakes! Invite students to keep their Word-a-Cognition sheets in their reading folders for learning reinforcement or to record new words.

Inclusion Tip

Read individually with all students, not just those who are classified. Spend about three to five minutes listening to each student read. If time is an issue, have students read into a tape recorder, first identifying the page number and paragraph from the text. Communicate reading gains on Word-a-Cognition sheets with parents during conferences.

Following are some commonly confused words:

accept	except	angel	angle
bought	brought	cease	seize
coma	comma	costume	custom
delay	daily	desert	dessert
device	devise	expect	suspect
loose	lose	personal	personnel
precede	proceed	quiet	quit/quite
started	stared	then	than

Word-a-Cognition

Directions: Record the words and phrases you read.

Date	Word/Phrase I Read	Correct Word/Phrase

Reading Templates

Reading can be a complex process for students whose brains are not automatically wired to read. An eclectic approach to reading features both word identification and reading comprehension skills. The following reading templates will help students sharpen their skills in phonological awareness, word decoding and encoding, structural analysis, context clues, reading comprehension, and writing.

Reproduce the following reading templates and staple them together to create a booklet for each student. Templates can be completed independently or in reading circles.

Inclusion Tip

Introduce template booklets by having all students read the same book and complete templates as a class, summarizing chapters and choosing vocabulary together. Afterward, groups can read different leveled books, and then simultaneously work on the same skills at their own reading levels.

Story Stuffer (page 22) It is easier for students to make sense of a story if they can break it down and organize the parts. When students read a story, they can "stuff" their ideas about it into the organizer. Students can write words, phrases, simple sentences, or page numbers where the information can be found. This organizer reinforces story elements: characters, setting, plot climax, and resolution.

Vocabulary Review (page 23) Students use this sheet to write definitions of chosen story vocabulary, sentences from the story using the words, and students' own sentences showing word meaning. This sheet helps reinforce meaning and spelling of unknown words and is great for test review.

Chapter Summaries (page 24) This sheet helps students learn to summarize storylines. Students list the main idea of each chapter in three to five well-constructed, detailed sentences. This also works as an excellent reference for test review while meaningfully connecting reading and writing skills.

Grade Your Book (page 25) This sheet gives students the opportunity to grade a book, chapter by chapter. Sometimes it takes more than one or two chapters to get involved in a book. This is an effective way to keep students from dismissing a book before they've given it a chance.

Name _____ Date _____

Story Stuffer

Directions: Write about a story you read in the boxes.

Characters (Who?)

Setting (Where? When?)

Plot/Climax (How did it happen? What's the problem? What's the exciting part?)

Resolution (Tell about the ending.)

Vocabulary Review

Directions: Write vocabulary words and their definitions.

1. Word: _____

Definition: _____

2. Word: _____

Definition: _____

3. Word: _____

Definition: _____

Directions: Write sentences from the story that use these vocabulary words.

1. _____

2. _____

3. _____

Directions: Write your own sentences using these vocabulary words.

1. _____

2. _____

3. _____

Chapter Summaries

Directions: Write a summary of each chapter in the boxes below.

Story Title: _____

Author: _____

Chapter _____

Chapter _____

Chapter _____

Name _____ Date _____

Grade Your Book

Directions: When you finish each chapter of a book, write the chapter number and date under the graph. Then grade the chapter, from 10 to 100, according to Grading Key.

Book Title: _____

Author: _____

Great	100				
Great	90				
Good	80				
Good	70				
Okay	60				
Okay	50				
Not Sure	40				
Not Sure	30				
Yuck	20				
Yuck	10				

Chapter _____ Chapter _____ Chapter _____ Chapter _____

Date _____ Date _____ Date _____ Date _____

Reading Quartets

Divide the class into groups of four, or reading quartets. These groups will work together to review stories they read in class. Keep these groups throughout the year, or form new groups each month, depending on the books chosen.

Assign one of the following books or another grade-appropriate favorite to each quartet. Tell group members to choose a role to play after reading the book, and then discuss their reading.

Connector: Tells how the book relates to other readings, writings, or his or her own life.

Asker: Thinks of questions prompted by the story and begins dialogue, promoting conversation.

Teller: Retells favorite, funny, sad, or interesting parts of the story.

Artist: Illustrates favorite scenes or characters from the book.

Inclusion Tip

Students with behavioral and attention issues will need more direction and supervision during cooperative reading quartets. Give frequent praise for time on task and appropriate social interactions.

Some Grade-Appropriate Books

Amber Brown Wants Extra Credit by Paula Danziger

Babe and Me: A Baseball Card Adventure by Dan Gutman

Because of Winn-Dixie by Kate DiCamillo

The Boy Who Owned the School by Gary Paulsen

Goalkeeper in Charge by Matt Christopher

Gooney Bird Greene by Lois Lowry

In the Year of the Boar and Jackie Robinson by Bette Bao Lord

Knights of the Kitchen Table by Jon Scieszka

Lily's Crossing by Patricia Reilly Giff

Ramona Forever by Beverly Cleary

The Storm by Cynthia Rylant

Train to Somewhere by Eve Bunting

Wanted . . . Mud Blossom by Betsy Byars

SOAR into Reading

SOAR into Reading pragmatically translates effective educational research about good teaching practices while motivating learners through differentiated instruction and the multiple intelligences. It is designed to help all students become actively and cooperatively involved in learning.

Multiple learning stations allow learners to choose their best way of understanding reading concepts as they circulate around the classroom to complete a variety of tasks. Some students may find the assignments too difficult, while others may need more challenges. For example, the Word Station could be modified to require fewer words for the word search, or you could use a larger font. Or, you could assign the acrostic just to students who need an extra challenge. Even though students work together, all are responsible for the finished product.

Invite students to work in groups of four. Different stations will play to individual student strengths. By asking groups to work together, all students will get the chance to make a contribution according to their talents and intelligences.

To begin, give students a copy of the **SOAR into Reading and Main Ideas and Details reproducibles (page 28 and 29)**. The first sheet provides students with tips on how to approach and review text before reading. The second sheet asks students to list main ideas and details from the reading to provide a deeper understanding of the text.

Then send out student groups to the following stations:

- **"Picture This!" Station (page 30):** illustrate main ideas

- **Word Station (pages 31–32):** create a word search, pantomime words, word acrostics

- **Testing Station (page 33):** design a test based on the reading

- **Performance Station (page 34):** create a skit, poem, song, commercial, video game, or dance about the reading

- **Research Station (page 35):** find out more about specific topics using resources such as computers, encyclopedias, and the library

Inclusion Tip

Keep track of the stations students choose, and encourage them to stretch their limits by attempting others. Stations can be used to demonstrate or review knowledge for nonfiction, science, and social studies texts and concepts as well as literature read throughout the school year.

SOAR into Reading

Directions: Use the SOAR method to help you get the most out of your reading.

Scan

Look at the titles, pictures, bold and highlighted words, charts, graphs, and other features in your book.

Outline

Read only the titles and headings of each section or chapter to determine the main ideas. Write the main ideas in your "Main Ideas and Details" Chart.

Analyze

You are not ready to read yet. Think about how the pictures, charts, vocabulary, and other features relate to those main ideas. Get a general understanding of your topic.

Read

Now, you are finally ready to read because you have previewed your topic!

After you finish reading, fill in the details in your Main Ideas and Details Chart. The reading will now make a lot more sense. Then fill in the You section of the chart, telling how you felt about the reading and how it relates to you.

After you have completed the "Main Idea and Details" Chart, further explore the book by going to each of the following stations:

- "Picture This!" Station

- Word Station

- Testing Station

- Performance Station

- Research Station

Name _____ Date _____

Main Ideas and Details

Directions: Use the chapter or section headings to help outline the main ideas. Read the words under these headings to find important details. Create a main idea organizer on a separate sheet of paper by copying the one below. Make as many organizers as you need for the reading selection. After the organizer, write your thoughts.

Book Title: _____

Page Numbers/Chapter/Section: _____

Main Ideas: Look at the titles and headings of each chapter and section.

Details: Read the selection to find details about each main idea.

You: Did you like the reading? Can you connect it to something you've learned before? Did it remind you of anything?

"Picture This" Station

Directions: Draw pictures of concepts from your reading that show more details about the main ideas. Refer to your Main Ideas and Details Chart. Write a caption for each picture.

Divide up the reading so that each student illustrates a different idea. Cut out and glue your pictures onto sheets of construction paper to make an illustration scrapbook.

Illustrator: _____

Caption: _____

_____

_____

Other ways to illustrate ideas include:

- Painting a picture
- Making a poster
- Creating an advertisement

- Making a collage
- Drawing a comic strip

Name _____ Date _____

Word Station 1

Directions: Choose ten vocabulary words from your reading, and write them on the lines. Then make a word search in the graph below. Exchange your word search with another group to solve. Take turns acting out your words for classmates to guess.

1. _____

2. _____

3. _____

4. _____

5. _____

6. _____

7. _____

8. _____

9. _____

10. _____

Word Station 2

An acrostic is a poem or sentences in which each line begins with the letter in a chosen word. Read the following acrostic based on the word **America**.

All people in America are free.

Make any choices you want for your life.

Elections are held so we can vote for our leaders.

Red and white stripes and 50 stars decorate our flag.

Immigrants from all over the world come to America.

Courageous people fought for our freedom.

Always be proud to be an American!

Directions: Choose two vocabulary words from your word search. On a separate sheet of paper, make an acrostic for each word that further explains or describes its meaning. You can use words, phrases, or sentences to express your ideas.

Word: _____   Word: _____

Acrostics Writers:

_____   _____

_____   _____

Testing Station

Directions: Now you are the teacher! On a separate sheet of paper, write a test based on your reading. You can use the following question starters to help you. When you are finished, exchange tests with another group.

Write the test

- Vary the types of questions. Write short answer and long answer questions. A *short answer* question can be answered with one or two words. A *long answer* question requires an explanation or description.

- Include questions that ask what, where, how, and why.

- Vary your questions by including:

True/False	Multiple Choice
Essay	Matching

- Create an answer key by writing the answers on a separate sheet of paper.

- Decide the score (points given for a correct answer) for each question. The total test score should add up to 100.

Sample Questions

Short answer question: *What is the story's setting?*

Long answer question: *Why do you think the main character changed her mind?*

Performance Station

Directions: Choose one of the following activities to perform with your group. Your performance should show ideas and concepts from the reading. It's your chance to make words come alive! Be creative!

Check the performance you chose.

☐ Write and perform a short skit.

☐ Write and perform a television commercial.

☐ Write and read aloud a poem.

☐ Sing a song or perform a rap.

☐ Create a board game or video game.

☐ Perform a dance.

☐ Write and perform jokes.

Use all available classroom resources such as:

- digital cameras
- tape recorders
- dictionaries and encyclopedias
- computers
- thesauruses
- CD players

Performers:

_____   _____

_____   _____

Name _____ Date _____

Research Station

Directions: Use classroom and library resources such as computers, encyclopedias, and almanacs to find more facts and details about the book or story you read. If you are using a computer, print out related information and highlight important facts to share with the class.

We learned these facts from our research:

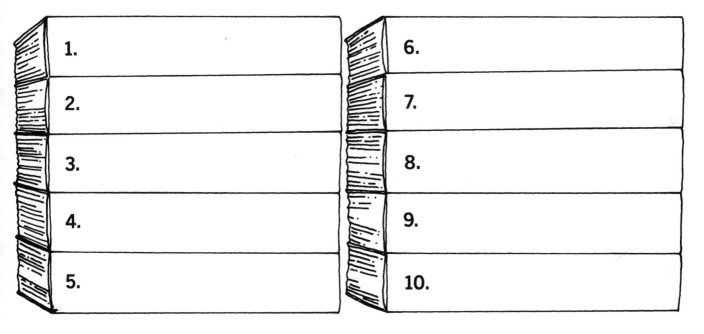

1.

2.

3.

4.

5.

6.

7.

8.

9.

10.

Materials used:*

_____

_____

_____

_____

*Sources must be correctly cited using bibliography guidelines.

Research conducted by:

_____   _____

_____   _____

CHAPTER 2

Writing

As students move into higher grades, they can become hesitant to write their thoughts on paper. Seeing corrections can be a frustrating, discouraging experience. Students must understand that writing is a form of communication that they can edit and improve. They can write about anything—their thoughts, stories, poems, letters, journals, and more!

Talking on Paper

Students must be motivated to write. Ask students, *How many of you like to talk with your friends?* Explain that writing is simply a way of "talking" on paper. Writing allows them to express their thoughts and ideas, just as they would in a conversation with friends.

Give students a copy of the **What Would It Say? reproducible (page 37)**. Tell them to use their imagination to think of what each object might say. Use this activity to reinforce punctuation as well, including the proper use of commas and periods with quotation marks. The recognition of writing as a form of communication is essential!

Inclusion Tip

Invite students to personalize this activity by drawing their own animate or inanimate characters that speak. They can also use magazine cutouts and computer clip art.

The Writing Process

Writing is a five-step process that includes thinking of a topic, writing a rough draft, revising, editing, and publishing. Give students a copy of **The Writing Process and Ed's Car reproducibles (pages 38–40)**. Read the text with students and answer any questions they may have. Reinforce the fact that writing is a process. The rough draft is only the first step in that process, and that draft must be reviewed and revised to make it better. Invite students to put these sheets in their writing folders as references. You may also choose to enlarge and post them around the classroom.

Inclusion Tip

Have students mark every other line on their papers as a reminder to skip lines in their rough drafts. This leaves ample room for editing.

Name _____ Date _____

What Would It Say?

Directions: Look at each object. What do you think the object would say if it could talk? Write a quotation on the line. Use quotation marks correctly.

1. _____
_____

2. _____
_____

3. _____
_____

4. _____
_____

5. _____
_____

6. _____
_____

7. _____
_____

8. _____
_____

The Writing Process

Good writing is a five-step process. Each step is important to making your writing the best it can be!

1. PREWRITING

Think about what you will write. Use an outline, graphic organizer, or list to organize your thoughts and ideas.

Here are some good places to find ideas:

- books, magazines, and newspapers
- conduct an interview
- electronic media (radio, TV, Internet)
- experiences
- movies
- music
- art (observing or creating)
- dreams

- memories
- discussion and brainstorming
- responding to literature
- role-playing
- research
- imagination
- personal interest inventories
- class interest inventories

2. WRITING

Use a pencil to write a rough draft. It doesn't need to be perfect. Just write down all your thoughts and ideas as they come to you. Let your ideas flow! Always skip lines so you can come back and make changes later.

3. REVISING

Writing means rewriting. When you're done with your rough draft, look back at what you have written. Think about how you can make it better. Ask yourself these questions:

- Is my writing clear?
- Does it make sense?
- Could I add more details to make my writing more interesting?
- Is the information in logical order?

The Writing Process

Use ED'S CAR to revise your writing. Refer to the ED'S CAR handout.

4. EDITING

Now that you've revised your writing, edit it!
Editing means looking for errors such as:

- punctuation
- spelling
- capitalization
- sentence structure
- subject/verb agreement

This step is a great time to share your writing with a classmate. Ask someone to read your writing and make suggestions for editing.

5. PUBLISHING

Your writing is at its best and ready for classroom publication! You can write your final draft neatly in ink or use a computer. Make your writing look as neat and clean as possible.

ED'S CAR

Expand

Write a simple sentence. Then make it longer by asking *who*, *what*, *when*, *where*, *why*, and *how* questions.

Expand this sentence: *The dog ran.*

- *Who* ran with the dog?
- *What* kind of dog was it?
- *When* did the dog run?
- *Where* did the dog run?
- *Why* did the dog run?
- *How* did the dog run?

New sentence: *The huge black dog ran quickly across the yard to greet me.*

Delete

Take away extra words that say the same thing.

Delete some words: *I went to the museum, and I went to the beach.*

New sentence: *I went to the museum and the beach.*

Substitute

Replace words with more specific, interesting words. Look for overused words like *said, happy, sad, fast, slow, big,* and *little.*

Substitute and delete some words: *The happy boy was happy because he won a contest.*

New sentence: *The boy was thrilled because he won the spelling bee.*

Combine And Rearrange

Combine and rearrange the words: *I live in the United States, and my country is the United States.*

New sentence: *The country where I live is the United States.*

Picture the Story

If pictures are worth a thousand words, than visuals can help ignite students' imagination! Give students a copy of the **Picture the Story reproducible (page 42)**. Invite them to write a detail describing the picture in each box. Inspire ideas by asking students: *What is the person doing? Where is the person going? How does the person feel?*

Then tell them to choose the picture they like best. They will build a short story around this character. Tell them to think of more characters, a setting, a plot, and an ending to this story. List the ideas below on chart paper for student reference. They can use these ideas or think of their own. When students are finished with their stories, group together those who chose the same picture. Invite them to share their stories with each other, comparing and contrasting ideas.

Inclusion Tip

If students have visual impairments, allow them an opportunity to write about tactile and auditory stimuli, describing the sounds and textures of those sensory prompts.

Characters	Settings	Plots/Themes	Endings
happy	beach	friendship	happiness
sad	desert	love	satisfaction
anxious	forest	thriller	partnership
excited	school	sports	compromise
funny	park	cooperation	winning
surprised	sports arena	adventure	sadness
angry	home	confidence	discovery

Picture the Story

Directions: Write details in the chart to describe each picture.

Detail 1					
Detail 2					
Detail 3					

Writing Planners

Writing planners, or graphic organizers, help students organize their thoughts around a central topic. They allow students to sort through and select ideas before writing them down.

Persuasive Writing Planner (page 44)

Ask students to use this planner to give reasons for and support their argument. After they have completed the planner, have them go back to edit their ideas, revising, deleting, and reorganizing as necessary. Then have students write out their essays on a separate sheet of paper, using the planner as a reference. Invite students to use their essays in a class debate on certain topics.

Sensory Writing Planner (page 45)

Descriptive writing is more vivid and interesting if students refer to what they see, hear, smell, touch, and taste. Words that appeal to the senses paint a more detailed picture for the reader. This planner helps students add sensory elements to stories or descriptive writing. Some students might begin by writing sentences that describe only one sense and location at a time (e.g., hearing a marching band in a parade, seeing a dinosaur in a museum). Later on, they can string sensory elements together to include other senses.

Well-Planned Writing: A Balanced Meal (pages 46–47)

This planner is designed to whet students' appetites for the written word. The familiar analogy of a well-balanced meal helps students make the connection to the building blocks of good writing. The next step is for students to use their ideas in a rough draft with sequential sentences and logical paragraphs.

Reflecting on My Writing (pages 48–49)

This crucial worksheet is intended to improve students' written work. The three levels of review—self, peer, and teacher—are all allies on a mission to reflect on and improve writing skills.

Inclusion Tips

If handwriting or fine motor skills present difficulties, allow students to dictate their ideas and thoughts to a scribe, or invite them to use tape recorders.

Be aware of quieter or possibly depressed students who may be reaching out for recognition and responses to their written communication.

Persuasive Writing Planner

Directions: Use this planner to help you write a persuasive essay. Make sure to give reasons and examples to support your argument.

1st Paragraph: Introduction

(State your argument.) I think _____

(State first reason.) First, _____

(State second reason.) In addition, _____

(State third reason.) Also, _____

2nd Paragraph (Expand on first reason; give an example.)

3rd Paragraph (Expand on second reason; give an example.)

4th Paragraph (Expand on third reason; give an example.)

5th Paragraph (Sum up all three reasons; restate your argument.)

Name _____ Date _____

Sensory Writing Planner

Directions: Use this planner to write sensory words for your essay or story.

Place or Setting	See	Hear	Smell	Touch	Taste

A Balanced Meal

Directions: Use this organizer to help you plan for writing.

1st Paragraph: Introduce your topic or story. Tell what it is about without giving specific details. This paragraph should briefly explain to the reader what you will write about. Answer these questions:

Who? _____

What? _____

When? _____

Where? _____

Why? _____

How? _____

A P P E T I Z E R

2nd Paragraph: Tell the reader what happens next. Think about the main idea of the paragraph, and then add more details.

Main Idea: _____

Details:

1. _____

2. _____

3. _____

4. _____

5. _____

6. _____

7. _____

S O U P

A Balanced Meal

3rd Paragraph

Main Idea: _____

Details:

S
A
L
A
D

1. _____

2. _____

3. _____

4. _____

5. _____

4th Paragraph

Main Idea: _____

Details:

E
N
T
R
E
E

1. _____

2. _____

3. _____

Conclusion

Ultimately,   Finally,
To summarize,   Looking back,

D
E
S
S
E
R
T

_____

Name _____ Date _____

Reflecting on My Writing

Directions: Use this chart to reflect on the writing.

Date	Reviewer	Title of Work	Comments/Suggestions/Reflections

Name _____ Date _____

Reflecting on My Writing (cont.)

Directions: Use these questions to help you reflect on the writing.

Questions to Think About

1. Were thoughts clearly stated?

2. Is the writing well organized?

3. Were words repeated? Should other words be substituted? Was the same thought or concept repeated using different words?

4. Did the writing flow with transition words such as *first*, *next*, *after*, *later*, or *finally*, helping the reader know that a new thought is coming?

5. Did each paragraph have a separate thought with its own main idea and supporting details? Were sentences choppy? Could some sentences be combined?

6. Were there spelling errors?

7. Is capitalization and punctuation correct?

8. Did you like writing and reading the piece? Why?

9. Do you understand what you just wrote and read?

CHAPTER 3

Mathematics

Math is vital for developing critical thinking skills across the curriculum. Math is not just adding and subtracting; it also includes conceptual lessons such as estimating, visualizing, deducing, and recognizing patterns. Math helps students in everyday, real-life situations such as averaging test scores, shopping, making change, telling time, measuring, and more.

Math Acrostics

An acrostic is a poem or sentences in which each line begins with the letter in a chosen word. Share the following math acrostic with students:

Math is a way of thinking.

Architects, engineers, cashiers, waiters, teachers, parents, and students use math every day!

There are rules for the way we add, subtract, multiply, and divide.

Hexagons, pentagons, and octagons are all polygons.

Each number has a value.

Multiplying is like repeated addition.

Adding results in a sum.

Telling time is math too!

Integers are whole numbers.

Counting correctly is important!

Subtraction is the opposite of addition.

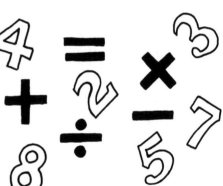

   Have students write their own math acrostics! They can use one of the following words or think of one of their own: *addition, subtraction, multiplication, division, fractions, ratios, geometry, money, percent.*

Inclusion Tip

Before students begin this activity, check to see if their word is spelled correctly. This is a perfect time to introduce a glossary. Make sure students include concepts related to their word. Afterward, bind students' acrostics into a class math book for all to share.

Logic Boxes

Math develops logical reasoning and thinking skills that can be transferred across the curriculum. Logic boxes are a great way to help students approach word problems that include critical thinking and breaking down information. Use this simple tool over and over again to help students organize information to solve problems.

Inclusion Tip

It is imperative that introduction to logic boxes be modeled on an overhead or the board before students attempt using them on their own. This help to avoid frustration and misunderstanding directions. Encourage more advanced learners to create their own logic problems and personalize them with a topic of interest.

Math Wheels

In order to be successful mathematicians, students must have command of basic addition, subtraction, multiplication, and division facts. That means being able to respond to facts quickly using "mental math." The **Math Wheels reproducible (page 52)** can be used repeatedly by varying the sign and numbers in the concentrically divided circles to teach and reinforce basic math skills.

Inclusion Tip

Have students review math facts by making flashcards. To add a visual component, students can shade in horizontal and vertical rows on graph paper that symbolize and further strengthen math concepts.

Math Wheels

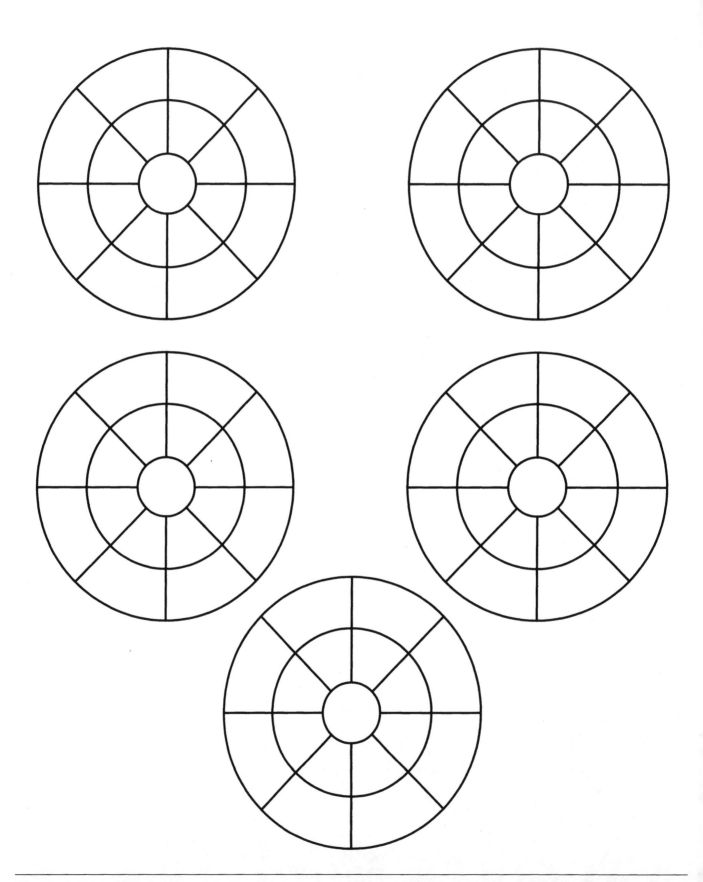

Write It, Show It, Know It!

Students with perceptual difficulties sometimes cannot distinguish between similar looking words and numbers. Use the **Write It, Show It, Know It! reproducible (page 54)** to give students the opportunity to see side-by-side comparisons of number words, numerals, decimals, and representative pictures. For more auditory cues, students can say each number aloud before and after they are written. Seeing the picture helps, too!

Nine-tenths = .90 = 9/10

Inclusion Tip

Invite students to use manipulatives such as fraction circles or decimal blocks to further concretize abstract concepts.

Signs and Symbols

Students may struggle with math concepts, not because of their lack of math knowledge, but due to visual, perceptual, processing, or reading errors. While quickly reading a problem, they might interpret the operation sign incorrectly, causing them to add or multiply instead of subtracting as the sign might indicate. Careful interpretation of decimals, place value, and operation symbols must be clear before problems can be correctly solved.

Give students a copy of the **Read the Signs reproducible (page 55)**. This activity is designed to increase student awareness of the crucial importance of concentrating, reading carefully, and understanding the language of math through its varied words and symbols.

Inclusion Tip

Encourage students to highlight or circle operation signs on math worksheets before they solve problems.

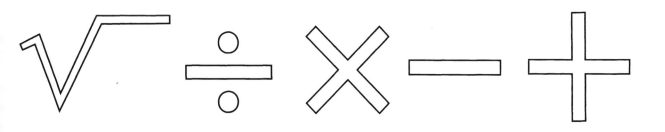

Write It, Show It, Know It!

Directions: Complete the chart below by writing the decimals and fractions, and then drawing pictures to show the number. The first one is done for you.

Words	Decimal	Fraction	Picture
1. one-half	.5	$\frac{1}{2}$	D
2. two-thirds			
3. six-eighths			
4. five-fifths			
5. two and two-thirds			

Directions: Now, look back at each number above. Look at the picture. Draw an X in the column that describes each number.

Less Than 1 Whole	1 Whole	More Than 1 Whole
1.		
2.		
3.		
4.		
5.		

Read The Signs

Directions: Math communicates with numbers and signs. Read each problem carefully. Then, match it with the correct description by circling A or B.

1. $3.00 < $30.00
   A. three dollars is less than thirty dollars
   B. three dollars is greater than thirty dollars

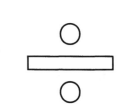

2. 18% = .18
   A. eighteen cents equals eighteen hundreds
   B. eighteen percent equals eighteen hundredths

3. n + 5 = 15
   A. fifteen added to five equals a number
   B. five added to a number equals fifteen

4. .25 + n = 1.00
   A. twenty-five hundredths plus a number equals one
   B. twenty-five hundredths plus a number equals one hundredth

5. (96 − n) 10 = 9
   A. ninety-six minus a number multiplied by ten equals nine
   B. ninety-six divided by a number minus ten equals nine

6. 20 − n = 2
   A. two subtracted from a number equals twenty
   B. a number subtracted from twenty equals two

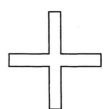

7. n ÷ 10 = 5
   A. a number divided by ten equals five
   B. a number plus ten equals five

8. 32 x .8 = n
   A. thirty-two multiplied by eight tenths equals a number
   B. thirty-two multiplied by eight equals a number

Strategies for Word Problems

Students may have difficulty knowing how to approach and solve word problems. Sometimes they need a step-by-step, systematic approach to help them break down the problem, sort through the information, and get to the "meat" of the math. The **Working Out Word Problems reproducible (page 57)** will help students learn a simple, logical way to approach word problems.

Write the following list on chart paper:

1. Read the word problem once.

2. Now read the word problem again to make sure you understand the question.

3. Write down the information you need in the data box.

4. Write the question you need to answer in the question box.

5. Draw an *X* or put a penny in the strategy box you have chosen.

6. Using a step-by-step approach, figure out the answer to the question.

7. Go back to the question box. Does your answer make sense?

Model for students how to complete each step. Draw a data box and question/answer box for students to see.

Data Box

Question
Answer

Show students how to use the Working Out Word Problems reproducible. Encourage students to use this approach on other word problems.

Developing Critical Thinking Skills

Math manipulatives, such as toothpick designs, tangram shapes, fraction pizzas, abacuses, flashcards, Unifix® cubes, algebra tiles, and more, help create concrete examples of abstract concepts that develop critical thinking skills.

The objective of the following activities, **Tricky Toothpicks (page 58)**, and **Techno Tangrams (page 59)**, is to have students analyze what they are doing, use logical sequencing, and kinesthetically imprint learned concepts. Students are asked to draw inferences using toothpicks and tangrams to develop deductive and inductive reasoning, spatial relationships, and cause-and-effect relationships. Strategies such as these can be transferred to inferential reading comprehension and various cognitive skills across the curriculum.

Name _____ Date _____

Working Out Word Problems

Directions: Choose a strategy to solve a word problem.

Estimate *It's about _____ .* *(28 is almost 30)*	**Guess and Check** 	**Draw a Picture**
Make a List 	**Break it into Parts** 	**Create a Chart or Table** 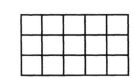
Look for a Pattern 2, 4, 6, 8, 10...	**Work Backward** 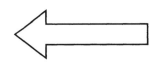	**Act It Out** 
Use Logical Reasoning 	**Solve a Simpler Problem** *How can I make this easier?*	**Set up an Equation** $A + B = C$ $C - B = A$

Tricky Toothpicks

Directions: Start by placing 12 toothpicks as shown below. Use them to make the shapes described below. Think carefully as you picture each shape in your head, and then make each shape. Remember, there is a difference between the words *move* and *remove*. Hint: Always return toothpicks to their original position before making a new shape.

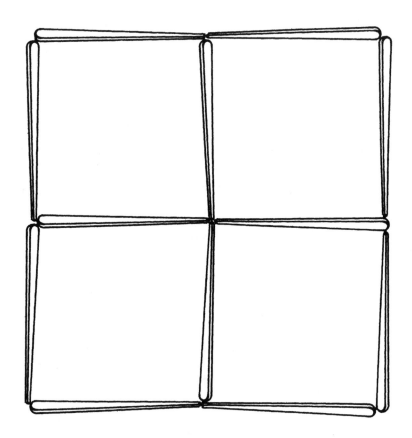

1. Move 2 toothpicks to make 7 squares.

2. Move 4 toothpicks to make 10 squares.

3. Remove 2 toothpicks to make 2 squares.

4. Move 3 toothpicks to make 3 squares.

Techno Tangrams

Directions: Cut apart the tangram shapes on this page. Use all seven shapes to make a square.

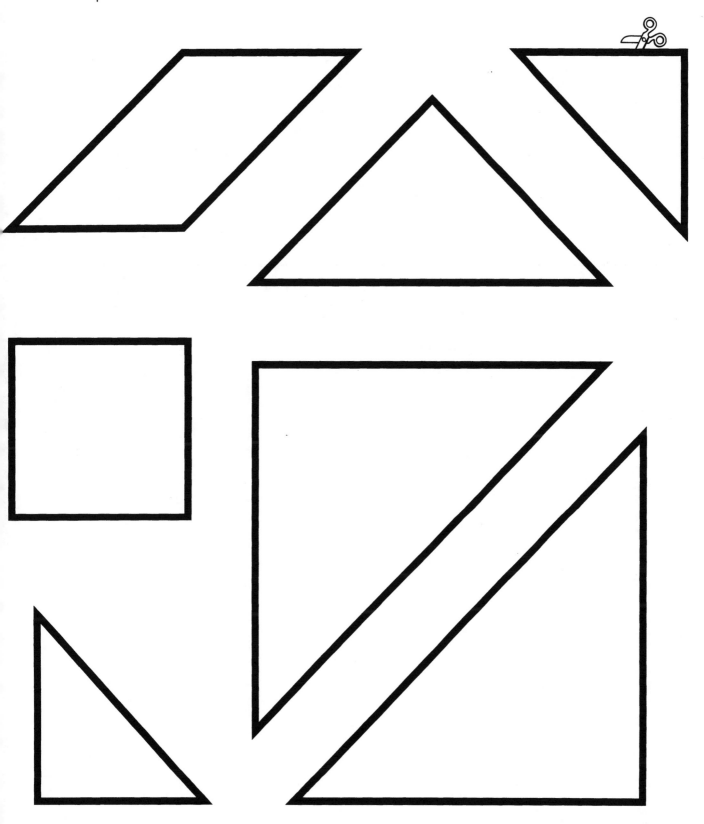

CHAPTER 4

Connecting Students to the Curriculum

Although specific standards must be met in each grade, teachers should first reach students on a level they can understand and form relationships. Subjects such as math, science, reading, art, music, physical education, and social studies can be connected to each other and tied to students' lives in meaningful ways. Teaching elementary students how to relate to concepts across the curriculum plants seeds for important adult skills such as multi-tasking, thinking analytically, and applying learning to a multitude of events and situations.

My Favorite Things

Begin your school year with an interest inventory to find out more about students' individual likes and dislikes. Give students a copy of the **My Favorite Things reproducible (page 61)** on the first day of school. After they have filled out the page, collect and file the pages for future reference. At the end of the school year, ask students to fill out the reproducible again to see if their choices stayed the same or changed.

Refer to students' choices in order to infuse their interests into the curriculum. For example, for a unit on world cultures, ask students to tell from where their ancestors came and some of the special cultural events they share with their families. Activities such as these motivate students, personalize the learning, and increase understanding.

Inclusion Tip

Concrete learners and those with lower literacy skills may have to dictate their thoughts to a classmate or class helper. As another option, students can cut out pictures from magazines or tie in technology with computer clip art.

Name _____   Date _____

My Favorite Things

Directions: What do you like? Draw a picture or write a few words inside each box to tell about your favorite things. Share your ideas with classmates.

Food	Person	Place
Book	Movie	TV Show
Season	Pet	Sport/Game
Song	Subject	Hobby

Different Ways of Learning

Saying that students learn differently within the multiple intelligences is really just another way of saying that each student is unique! Self-awareness of likes and dislikes is important for young learners. You should also be aware of your own preferred (stronger) and weaker intelligences. If you do not like a subject, you might subliminally send out negative messages to students, such as *I don't like or feel comfortable with this topic.* All intelligences and students have value!

Give students a copy of the **Different Ways of Learning reproducible (page 63)**. Invite them to look at the pictures and think about which activities they like best and least. Help students rank the activities by writing the numbers 1–8 in the boxes.

The multiple intelligences are labeled as follows:

- Verbal/Linguistic—Book Smart

- Interpersonal—People Smart

- Bodily/Kinesthetic—Body Smart

- Visual/Spatial—Picture Smart

- Logical/Mathematical—Number Smart

- Naturalistic—Nature Smart

- Intrapersonal—Self Smart

- Musical/Rhythmic—Music Smart

- Existential—Infinite/Philosophy Smart (Beyond what you see)

Inclusion Tip

To add kinesthetic and interpersonal elements, place signs and pictures around the room that portray the eight intelligences shown in the chart. Ask students to first go to their favorite station, and then go to their least favorite. Ask students to discuss thoughts with peers at that station. Post intelligences signs all year as reminders that it's okay to learn in different ways!

Different Ways of Learning

Directions: Look at the pictures in the boxes. Label all the boxes, from 1 to 8. Write 1 in the box that shows what you like to do best. Number your least favorite activity 8.

Book Smart Reading and writing	People Smart Working in groups and being with friends
Body Smart Dancing and sports	Picture Smart Putting pictures together
Self Smart Thinking and being by myself	Number Smart Math and computers
Nature Smart Being in nature	Music Smart Singing and playing musical instruments

Serving Up Geography

Movement gets students out of their seats and thinking on their feet! Serve up some knowledge by doing the following activity.

1. Write the following geography words on paper plates: *North America; Canada; Mexico; Pacific Ocean; Atlantic Ocean; Gulf of Mexico; Washington, DC; Philadelphia; South America; New York; Fifty; Thirteen; Mississippi.* Spread out the plates around the floor. (To increase difficulty, add more statements and "paper plate" answers.)

2. Have students stand in a circle and look at the paper plate choices as you read aloud the statements below.

3. Invite students who know the answer to raise their hand. Choose a student to jump on the paper plate answer. If the student is correct, he or she gets to keep the plate.

4. Read the following statements, one by one, until you are finished. The student with the most paper plates wins!

   - *The United States is on this continent.*

   - *This country borders the United States to the north.*

   - *This country borders the United States to the south.*

   - *This body of water is on the east coast of the United States.*

   - *This body of water is on the west coast of the United States.*

   - *This body of water is to the south of the United States.*

   - *This city is the capital of the United States.*

   - *This city is home to the Liberty Bell.*

   - *This city is home to the Statue of Liberty.*

   - *This the number of original colonies in the United States.*

   - *This is the number of states in the United States.*

   - *This is the longest river in the United States.*

5. Afterward, invite students to review world geography by establishing north, south, east, and west directions in the classroom (like a large compass rose). Ask students to review world continents and large bodies of water by placing paper plates in the correct geographic location in the room.

Inclusion Tips

If students have physical, visual, or auditory issues and cannot fully participate in this activity, allow them to assume a different but integral role, such as cartographer (handing out the plates), scorekeeper/plate counter, or checker (verifying answers against the answer key).

Students with lower cognitive levels can be graded on just one skill (e.g., identifying compass directions or bodies of water vs. landforms).

Chemistry in the Classroom

Chemistry is not just a science topic; it is also about everyday events and interactions with our environment. The purpose of this activity is to meaningfully relate and personalize these chemical concepts to students' lives.

Give students a copy of the **Matter and You reproducible (page 66)**. Have them read about the properties of matter, and provide several concrete examples such as:

- showing a moldy piece of bread

- burning a candle

- tearing a piece of paper

- mixing clay or paint

- melting ice

Placing each example into one of two boxes labeled *Chemical Changes* and *Physical Changes*. Invite students to think about how they interact with matter every day. What chemical or physical changes take place? Have students complete the reproducible.

Inclusion Tip

Invite students to keep a Chemistry Diary, deciding whether daily actions would fall in the physical or chemical category.

Matter and You

Directions: Study the chart below. Then read the sentences to decide whether a physical or chemical change occurs with each event. Write *P* for *physical* or *C* for *chemical* in the box before each statement.

Different Reactions

1. Matter is anything that takes up space and has mass.

2. Reactions or changes can be physical or chemical.

Physical Changes	Chemical Changes
• Different shape • Different color • Can change what it looks like: solid, liquid, gas	• Atoms rearrange • Different properties than original substance (liquid rather than a solid)

☐ **1.** Get dressed.

☐ **2.** The bread you were going to eat is green with mold.

☐ **3.** Instead, you'll have some scrambled eggs.

☐ **4.** Pour milk on your cereal.

☐ **5.** Squeeze some fresh orange juice to drink.

☐ **6.** You see a construction crew hammering nails to fix your roof.

☐ **7.** Your dad is mowing the lawn.

☐ **8.** Ahh, you smell fall leaves burning.

☐ **9.** You want to ride your bike to school, but the chain is rusted.

☐ **10.** When you get to school, you break your pencil.

CHAPTER 5

Comprehension and Study Skills

The time students spend in school is only the beginning of learning. Educators will acknowledge that the students who do best in class are those who also complete homework assignments on time and review learned concepts at home. It is important to instill these good study habits in young learners while encouraging the home-to-school connection.

The purpose of the following reproducibles is to increase student awareness of how efforts at home and school have positive consequences. They will realize that successful learning output does not occur spontaneously, but is related to the effort of their input. These reproducibles help to map the journey!

- **How Well Do You Study? (page 68)** asks students to honestly rate their study skills and test preparation strategies.

- **Following Directions (page 69)** is a class activity that reminds students to carefully review written directions before they plunge into an activity. In a rush to finish an activity, students often misread directions or just don't bother to read carefully. This activity reinforces the importance of careful reading and review.

- **Amazing Mnemonics (page 70)** provides students with an invaluable study and memory tool. First, familiar samples are provided, and then students are asked to create their own.

- **Tracking My Assignments (page 71)** encourages students to track their assignments and stay organized. This proactive skill is one that students will use throughout their lives as they advance academically and learn to juggle daily schedules.

Inclusion Tip

These activities are not just intended for one day of instruction, but should be modeled throughout the year. Good study skills develop and improve over time. Emphasize to students with behavioral issues, low self-esteem, and less parental support (who might need more positive "self-talk") that even though they may not have reached their goals yet, they are on the right track! Soon they will see results bloom, as they become active participants in control of their academic destiny.

How Well Do You Study?

Directions: Examine your study skills. You can always get better! Check all statements below that apply to you and your study skills.

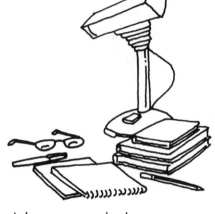

1. When do you review or read your textbooks or class notes?

   __ the night before a test

   __ in class only

   __ daily review at home and class

   __ never

2. Where do you do your homework?

   __ in a quiet place

   __ in the kitchen

   __ on the bus ride home from school

   __ other _____

3. Why do you study?

   __ parents give rewards

   __ it makes me feel good about myself to do well in school

   __ my parents force me

   __ other _____

4. How do you study for a test?

   __ while watching television

   __ use a study guide

   __ review/rewrite notes and textbook

   __ other _____

5. What do you think about school?

   __ it can help me later on in life

   __ it's boring

   __ it's a waste of time

   __ I love learning

Following Directions

Directions: This is a five-minute, timed exercise on different school topics. Read all the questions before you begin.

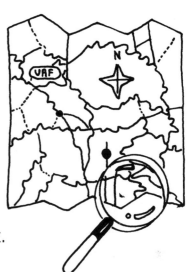

1. Write your name and the date at the top of the page.

2. Underline the word *exercise.*

3. Write all the odd numbers from 1 to 49.

4. List the seven continents in alphabetical order.

5. Write the lowercase alphabet in cursive or manuscript.

6. Draw a picture of something that is recyclable.

7. Write the title of your favorite book.

8. List five words that rhyme with school.

9. Write, "I love school!" twenty times.

10. Now that you have read everything, do numbers 1 and 2 only, and then patiently wait and watch classmates complete the worksheet.

Amazing Mnemonics

Words or short phrases that help you recall facts, rules, concepts, or information are called mnemonics. Mnemonics are a valuable study tool.

Directions: Do any of the following phrases ring a bell? Write what each mnemonic stands for on the line. (Ask your classmates for help.)

1. My **V**ery **E**ducated **M**other **J**ust **S**erved **U**s **N**uts

_____

2. HOMES

_____

3. Every **G**ood **B**oy **D**oes **F**ine

_____

4. SEAN got three **AAA**s.

_____

5. Please **E**xcuse **M**y **D**ear **A**unt **S**ally

_____

6. ROY G. BIV

_____

Directions: List your favorite mnemonics, or come up with some of your own!

1. _____

2. _____

3. _____

Name _____ Date _____

Tracking My Assignments

Directions: Do you have a hard time keeping track of your assignments and test dates? Use this sheet each day or week as a reminder of what you need to do.

Subject	Date Due	Books/Materials Needed	Done

Setting Learning Goals

Setting goals for learning is the first step in creating a foundation for good study habits. This activity will encourage students to think about how they approach learning and how to develop good study skills.

Give each student several copies of the **My Learning Goals reproducible (page 73)**. Go over each statement with the class and discuss the different strategies students can use to approach and learn new concepts and then reflect on their study habits.

To get started, help each student set one or two personal goals for learning or studying a specific topic (e.g., multiplication facts, spelling, reading). Then ask students to use their charts to help them achieve those goals. Each day, they will write Y for *yes*, N for *no*, or S for *sometimes* in the chart to show what they did that week to meet their goals.

Encourage students to continue to set learning goals throughout the year and keep track of what they do each week to achieve these goals.

Inclusion Tip

If the idea of a goal seems abstract, then create an analogy for students, such as sports (e.g., hockey or soccer goals), with the classroom as their playing field!

Name _____ Date _____

My Learning Goals

Directions: What did you do this week to reach your learning goal? For each statement, write Y for *Yes*, N for *No*, or S for *Sometimes*.

My Learning Goal: _____

	Monday	Tuesday	Wednesday	Thursday	Friday
I read about it.					
I heard about it.					
I asked questions.					
I practiced in class.					
I reviewed it at home.					
I asked a parent for help.					
I did my homework.					
I tried my best.					
I learned it!					

"Every Body" Can Learn!

This thematic, interdisciplinary "body unit" can be applied across the curriculum in a variety of creative ways. This unit depicts how a topic such as the human body can be explored and differentiated in a way that embraces the multiple intelligences.

Inclusion Tip

It is important that students develop positive self body images in the elementary grades and beyond. Discussion about bodies should reinforce that every body has equal worth, regardless of physical appearances or the way it may function. Always capitalize on strengths, not weaknesses.

Activities for Every Body Across the Curriculum

- **Theater Arts/Writing:** Have students create a writing planner listing different body parts. Then have student groups each create a play with a cast of body parts personified as the main characters! The writing planner could include body parts (e.g., *arms*), actions of the body parts (e.g., *lift* or *move*), and descriptions of those actions (e.g., *strong* or *quick*). "Arms" could become a play about a person winning a marathon using a wheelchair!

- **Reading/Decoding:** Invite students to associate body parts with initial or final consonant sounds of words. For example, if you are covering initial sounds, say words such as *house, hat,* and *hello.* Students then point to their *head.*

- **Science/Technology:** Have students learn about anatomy, medical advances, and proper care of the body by doing some research on the computer. Students could also compare the human body to different machines.

- **Math:** Ask students to measure hand spans, distances from knees to toes or shoulders to wrists, and circumference of heads. Measure their height in quarters, nickels, and dimes. Compare body ratios to increase knowledge of number sense, fractions, proportions, scales, and measurements. For example: Use a string to measure height, and then wrap that string around the circumference of the head. The ratio should be 3:1.

- **Art/Music/Dance:** Trace hands or feet to create abstract pictures. Sing "body" songs such as the Hokey-Pokey, or play a game such as Simon Says while playing background music.

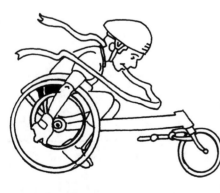

978-1-4129-5235-4

CHAPTER 6

Reflective Assessment, Testing, and Grading

In the past, learners with special needs were often removed from mainstream learning and placed in separate classes with lower requirements. Unfortunately, this resulted with many adults being ill prepared to meet societal demands.

Assessments take many shapes and forms. Grades can be obtained from portfolios, observations, paper or oral tests and quizzes, homework, reports, class projects and participation, and more. Students with special needs often do not fare well with typical assessments. Reasons for failure can vary from lower cognitive levels, poor or inappropriate instruction, and sometimes a lack of motivation and/or attention.

This situation calls for both you and the student to challenge your way of thinking. Ask yourself: *Is there another way I can teach this subject to this student?* Students should ask themselves: *Have I tried my best?* Both teachers and students should be involved in the assessment process.

Progress Chart

Students' efforts are usually commendable, but the grades achieved do not always reflect this progress. A progress chart allows them to chart and concretely assess their progress and achievements over time.

Give each student several copies of the **My Progress Chart reproducible (page 76)**. Invite students to write the subject they want to chart at the top of the page. (Consult with students individually to decide on an appropriate subject.) Each time they have a test in this subject, students can write the date and draw a dot on the appropriate line for the score. Over time, they will see how they have progressed or where they need improvement.

Inclusion Tip

Do not allow other students to distribute tests or papers. Remind students that it is not all about grades, but steps taken and improvements achieved. More advanced learners can benefit from this chart as well, since it regulates study habits. If a student does not put forth optimum effort, results on the graph will reflect that.

Name _____   Date _____

My Progress Chart

Directions: Plot each test score on the chart.

Subject: _____

My personal goal for this subject: _____

TEST SCORES															
100															
95															
90															
85															
80															
75															
70															
65															
60															
55															
50															
45															
40															
35															
30															
25															
20															
15															
10															
5															
Dates															

Show What You Know!

Teaching to the multiple intelligences is not just a theory; it should be implemented and practiced in every inclusive classroom. One way to embrace the multiple intelligences in your classroom is by allowing students to explore different ways to "show what they know," ways that differ from typical tests and assessments.

Make several copies of the **Show What You Know reproducible (page 78)** for each student. Throughout the school year, encourage students to try different ways to show what they've learned about various topics.

Inclusion Tip

Have students choose one method from the sheet to show what they know prior to taking a more conventional test. The knowledge gained will be appropriately transferred and retained!

Thinking About Learning

Learning does not take place overnight. Students should understand that learning is a process that can be continually honed, explored, and improved. There is no quick fix! When students reflect on what they've learned, they have the opportunity to see how they change and grow over time.

Give each student several copies of the **Thinking About Learning reproducible (page 79)**. As students are introduced to new concepts, invite them to fill out this sheet to reflect on their learning and make goals for the coming week and month. Have students keep these sheets in a folder so they can look back to see if they've met their weekly and monthly goals. These sheets are also great for test review!

Inclusion Tips

Encourage students with cognitive needs or organizational issues to record information on weekly or monthly desk, pocket, refrigerator, or wall calendars.

Students with communication challenges may need pictures and symbols that allow them to express their thoughts with visuals. Use a digital camera to take appropriate personalized classroom pictures and combine them with shared family photos from home.

Name _____ Date _____

Show What You Know!

Directions: How many different ways can you show what you know? Use this sheet to find different to show what you've learned.

To prove that I learned about _____, I will:
(Topic/Concept)

_____ write a play

_____ compose a song or jingle

_____ create a comic strip/cartoon

_____ make a video

_____ perform a dance

_____ complete a take-home test

_____ teach it to another student

_____ develop an experiment

_____ create a graph or chart

_____ create a sculpture with mixed media

_____ invent a product

_____ write an essay or poem

_____ write jokes on the topic

_____ create a Microsoft® PowerPoint® presentation

_____ keep a learning log

_____ work on a group project

_____ do a research report

_____ build a model

_____ write a newspaper article or editorial

_____ compile a scrapbook with computer clip art or my own art work

_____ design a game

_____ create a timeline of important events or details

_____ other _____

Agreed upon on _____ by:
(Date)

_____ and _____
(Student's Name)   (Teacher's Name)

Assignment will be completed by _____.
(Date)

Name _____ Date _____

Thinking About Learning

Directions: Use this sheet to review and write about what you've learned and to set future learning goals.

Yesterday I Learned:
Today I Learned:
My Goals for This Week:
My Goals for This Month:

Creating a Climate for Classroom Acceptance

Even if you have minimal experience instructing students with exceptionalities, you can still achieve successful inclusion for all students! First, establish a level of comfort and trust amongst you, the students, and their parents. Second, increase your knowledge of cognitive, behavioral, sensory, communication, physical, and learning differences through simulations, literature, and daily academic and social interactions. Most important, maintain a positive mindset, which most often yields positive and beneficial inclusion results.

Both younger and older students must increase their dis-ABILITY awareness. Accepting others should come naturally to all of us. However, in some cases, people with exceptionalities or differences are often the recipients of negative and unfounded perceptions and prejudices. In today's inclusive classrooms, students need help realizing that there are differences amongst all of us. These are the very things that make us special and unique! Through early training, students can learn to accept people as they really are and maximize the potential of who they can be. A positive classroom climate will create an atmosphere of acceptance where all individuals are valued!

Model appropriate inclusive etiquette and encourage students to role-play possible classroom scenarios to maximize not only academic, but also social opportunities for acceptance. The student reproducibles **We're All Individuals (page 81)**, **Thinking About Disabilities (page 82)**, and **Understanding Differences (page 83)** act as conduits that merit abilities, encourage reflections, and promote positive peer interactions. Walk through each activity with students, encouraging them to share their thoughts and feelings along the way. Students will realize that everyone has strengths and weaknesses. Remember to focus on their strengths!

Inclusion Tip

Don't force relationships if students are not compatible. Respect individual choices, with and without disabilities. Focus on self-esteem and confidence building activities. Students who feel good about themselves are less apt to put others down to build their own character.

We're All Individuals

Directions: Rate your personal strengths and weaknesses on this graph.

	Singing	Writing	Spelling	Dancing	Being a Friend	Drawing	Math	Sports
10								
9								
8								
7								
6								
5								
4								
3								
2								
1								

Thinking About Disabilities

Directions: Read these statements. Decide if you think they are true or false. Write *T* for *true* or *F* for *false* before each statement.

1. _____ Everyone has differences.

2. _____ We should treat someone with a disability the same way we would like to be treated.

3. _____ Don't be afraid to be yourself!

4. _____ We should be friends with someone with a disability if we like the person, not just because he or she has a disability. Pity helps no one!

5. _____ People and places can be the handicaps for someone with a disability.

6. _____ A sensitive, caring attitude helps people with disabilities.

7. _____ Disabilities do not define people. The disability is just a small part of the whole person.

8. _____ We should focus on people's strengths and abilities, not their weaknesses and disabilities.

Directions: Complete these sentences.

9. The base word of disability is _____ !

10. If a friend or family member had a dis-ABILITY, I would

_____

_____

_____

The lesson: All of these statements are true!

Understanding Differences

Directions: Try these activities to help you understand people with differences. Think about how you might feel if you couldn't perform tasks the same way or as easily as others.

1. Close your eyes during a class lesson. Try to imagine what other students are doing. Can you take notes? With your eyes still closed, ask a classmate to lead you around the classroom.

2. Cover your ears during a class a lesson. Look around the room at other students. Can you understand what is going on around you?

3. Read this sentence: mose dentsuts ees nights flyfiderent anth ouy od.

4. Try tying your shoes while you are wearing mittens.

5. Place your tongue on the roof of your mouth and say this sentence: Talking with my tongue on the roof of my mouth is very difficult!

Directions: Now, answer the following questions in your journal.

6. Which activity do you think was the most difficult?

7. How do you think someone who does things differently during school activities or at home feels about him or herself?

8. How do students look at or feel about a classmate with differences?

9. Would you like to try these activities again? Why or why not?

10. What have you learned?

We All Have Value

Everyone is valuable, no matter what his or her differences and abilities. Every student has special skills and talents. Sometimes we just need to be reminded that differences make us the unique individuals we are. The following activities will help students see the value in each other's differences.

To complete these activities, you will need the following materials:

- 3 empty coffee cans
- money (one-dollar bill, 4 quarters, 100 pennies)
- empty opaque, plastic juice bottle
- paper lunch bag
- bag or box of rice

1. Place the following items in three separate coffee cans: one-dollar bill, 20 pennies, and one quarter. Shake each can individually, and ask students: Which can do you think is worth more? The lesson here is that sometimes, valuable things are not easy to identify. What we hear or see on the outside does not tell the whole story!

2. Place the following items in three separate coffee cans: one-dollar bill, 100 pennies, and four quarters. Shake each can individually, and ask students: Which can do you think is worth more? The lesson here is that we don't always know what's on the inside by what we see or hear on the outside. In this case, the cans are all equal, but in different ways. People are equal in different ways too!

3. Place equal amounts of rice in a coffee can, a juice bottle, and a lunch bag. Shake each container individually, and ask students: What do you think is inside these containers? The lesson here is that even though something appears different on the outside, the contents are the same. Every person has the same worth, regardless of what he or she looks like on the outside. Discuss the phrase You can't judge a book by its cover.

4. Ask students: What do you think is worth more, rice or money? Discuss the concept of value with students. Lead them to realize that rice would be worth more to a starving person on a deserted island. This person would have no use for money. The lesson here is that each person has different needs.

Books That Embrace Differences

The following books help students increase their exposure and sensitivity to differing abilities. After reading a book, invite students to discuss the theme and concepts with a partner or in small cooperative groups. Students can draw pictures in a storyboard or PowerPoint presentation and discuss the characters, plot, and setting. Invite them to share what they learned in a kind and respectful way.

Blue Bottle Mystery: An Asperger Adventure by Kathy Hoopmann (Asperger Syndrome)

Different Like Me: My Book of Autism Heroes by Marc Thomas and Jennifer Elder (autism)

Hank Zipzer: The World's Greatest Underachiever—I Got a "D" in Salami by Henry Winkler and Lin Oliver (learning differences)

How to Behave and Why by Munro Leaf (character building, behavioral issues)

In Their Own Words: Helen Keller by George Sullivan (blindness, deafness, and courage)

Learning to Slow Down and Pay Attention: A Book for Kids About ADHD by Kathleen G. Nadeau, Ph.D. and Ellen B. Dixon, Ph.D. (ADHD)

Loser by Jerry Spinelli (learning differences)

Louis Braille: The Boy Who Invented Books for the Blind by Margaret Davidson (blindness)

Putting on the Brakes: Young People's Guide to Understanding Attention Deficit Hyperactivity Disorder by Patricia O. Quinn, M.D. and Judith M. Stern, M.A. (ADHD)

Special Brothers and Sisters: Stories and Tips for Siblings of Children with Special Needs, Disability, or Serious Illness edited by Annette Hames and Monica McCaffrey (various special needs)

Small Steps: The Year I Got Polio by Peg Kehret (physical differences)

The Summer of the Swans by Betsy Byars (sibling with a cognitive disability)

Thank you, Mr. Falker by Patricia Polacco (dyslexia)

There's a Boy in the Girls' Bathroom by Louis Sachar (behavioral issues)

Up and Down the Worry Hill: A Children's Book about Obsessive-Compulsive Disorder and Its Treatment by Aureen Pinto Wagner, Ph.D. (obsessive-compulsive disorder)

The Year of Miss Agnes by Kirkpatrick Hill (different type of classroom in Alaska)

Zipper: The Kid with ADHD by Caroline Janover (ADHD)

Parent Survey

Student's Name: _____

Parent's/Guardian's Name: _____

1. What does my child think about school?

   _____

2. What do I visualize my child doing in 10 or 15 years?

   _____

3. What are my child's special or individual needs?

   _____

4. Some words I would use to describe my child are:

   _____

5. What are my child's favorite things to do?

   _____

6. What would I change about my child's school or classroom experience?

   _____

7. What do I like about my child's school or classroom?

   _____

8. My areas of expertise that I could share with my child's class are:

   _____

9. I'd like to volunteer to help with:

   _____

10. You may contact me at:

   _____

Home: _____ Work: _____ Cell: _____

E-mail: _____

Home Address: _____

   _____

Charting Lessons

Use this chart to keep notes from IEPs you have read and monitor how lessons align with modifications and goals listed in the IEP.

Subject: _____   Teachers: _____

Modifications/Accommodations	
MBHE—Modified, but high expectations	**C/T**—Computer/technology
G—Grading modified	**M**—Alternative materials
S—Seating	**OW**—Oral/written presentations
HW—Homework modified/reduced	**MS**—Multisensory techniques
P—Preteaching	**CST**—Child study team support
R—Reteaching/repetition	**PI**—Parental involvement
A—Assessment varied/simplified	**B**—Buddy system
SG—Study guide	**NT**—Note-taking system
V—Visuals	**LOV**—Learning objective varied
T—Extra time, or wait time for tasks	**O+**—Other modifications
BP—Behavior plan	

Students	Modifications/ Accommodations	Assessments/Dates Mastery Level	Comments

ABCD Quarterly Checklist of Functional Objectives

Use these codes:

A = Always

B = Becoming better

C = Can do with reminders

D = Doesn't display behavior

Student Name: _____

OBJECTIVES	Q1	Q2	Q3	Q4
Establishes eye contact with teachers and peers				
Uses proper conversational tones				
Follows classroom and school rules				
Respects authority				
Exhibits social reciprocity				
Appropriately communicates needs				
Demonstrates consistent attention during classroom lessons				
Completes all classroom assignments				
Finishes all homework and long-range assignments				
Able to take class notes independently				
Writes legibly				
Keeps an organized work area				
Respects the property of others				
Works well with groups				
Adjusts to changes in routines				
Asks for clarification when needed				
Takes pride in achievements				
Displays enthusiasm about learning				

Student Referral Planner

WHY does this student need a referral? Is it for academic, behavioral, and/or social reasons? List the student's strengths and weaknesses on the reverse side of this planner.

WHO has been contacted? Is anyone currently seeing or supporting this child?

WHEN is a good time to observe this student?

WHAT strategies/implementations have you tried? Attach any documentation such as sample academic work, tests, or behavioral logs.

Student Referral Planner
(STOP and THINK)

HOW can the CST help?

WHERE is this student currently educated?

Curriculum Recording, Documentation, and Observations

Content Area: _____

Objectives: _____

_____

Student and/ or Dates	Student is able to fully participate in the same lesson as peers.	Student needs modified expectations and/or extra materials to accomplish lesson objectives.	Student can independently participate in a different but related assignment in the room.	Student cannot proficiently complete task in the classroom, even with support.	Brief comments, observations, needs, modifications, notes, V/A/K/T concerns, future plans

Classroom Structure to Promote Inclusion

Questions you might ask yourself

- How can classes teach the same topic while considering different levels of development and ability?

- What about classroom management?

- Can one teacher divide the class into focused groups?

It's simple, if you think about your classroom in the following ways:

- Everyone is learning together in one room.

- Different thought processes and levels (independent, instructional, frustrations) exist within the same room.

- Teaching everyone does not mean that students are learning the same breadth of material at the same time.

- The ultimate goal is progress for all based upon individual needs.

Suggestions for classroom structure

Think of how your lessons can be composed of the following three parts.

Everyone in the class could

Whole

- Listen to the same story, poem, mathematical word problem

- Look at the same picture prompt related to the content

- Chorally read or write a story together on chart paper

- Have a group discussion about the topic

- Be introduced to science and social studies vocabulary

- Preview and discuss on what skill(s) the lesson will focus (e.g., scientific method, timelines, decimals, finding the main idea, how to improve writing by substituting words)

- Be involved in a teacher demonstration or experiment, handling concrete objects or lesson-related manipulatives

Students can work with smaller groups, partners, or individually to:

Part

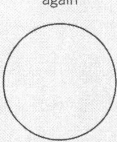

- Complete an assigned reading or writing task

- Create a product based upon what was learned (e.g., write a poem, story, or short skit; illustrate captioned pictures; solve a crossword puzzle, word search, or given problem; reenact an experiment; conduct research on the computer; read and learn more about the topic)

- Complete varying activities from a chapter, using matching colored paper (e.g. green, blue, yellow assignment) for better classroom management

- Complete learning tasks under teacher's auspices

During this time, walk around the classroom supervising or instructing smaller groups or individual students, while recording observations and individual needs evidenced.

Together the class becomes a whole unit again, while individual students, teachers, partners, and groups share:

Whole
again

- What else they learned or discovered about the topic from a book, computer, other student, teacher, or self

- A finished product created

- What they now know, giving specific details

- What they still wonder about

- Questions about the material presented

This is basically a time for all learners to celebrate their discoveries and progress with each other, while validating and reflecting upon their own learning.

978-1-4129-5235-4

Three-Question Lesson Design

Lesson design requires asking these three simple questions:

1. What are you going to teach? ————→ Objective

2. How are you going to teach it? ————→ Procedure

3. Did it work? ————→ Assessment

Special education can be special for everyone involved, if you consider the following factors. Remember, not every lesson requires all of these ingredients, but perhaps being cognizant of their importance will allow these objectives to evolutionarily diffuse into the repertoires of all teachers. Think about how the following points fit into your lessons:

- Topic

- Desired Goals (Social/Academic/Emotional/Physical/Cognitive)

- Baseline Knowledge

- Motivating Activity (Visual/Auditory/Kinesthetic-Tactile Sensory Elements)

- Critical/Creative Thinking Skills

- Interpersonal Activity/Cooperative Roles

- Curriculum Connections

- Possible Accommodations

- Parallel Activity

- Anticipated roles of General Educator/Special Educator/ Instructional Assistant/Student/Peers/Family/Specialists/Related Services

- Administration

- Adult/Peer/ Self Assessments

- Closure

- Revisitation Plans

Inclusive Reflections

Use this form to account for and take pride in both your own and your students' achievements and efforts. It is a speculative professional self-evaluation combined with an inclusive pedagogical student reflection. It shows where you and your students have been, where you are now, and where you are heading.

	YES	NO
Was this student's prior knowledge increased?		
Even though this student did not receive a passing grade (e.g., 50% on an evaluation), did he or she master 50% of the material?		
Do you think this student will be more proficient when he or she learns about this topic, content area, or skill again?		
Is there a way to repeat this learning and somehow individualize instruction within the classroom (e.g., alternate assignment on the same topic) if appropriate support is given, such as a parent, peer coach, or paraeducator?		
Would assigning a peer coach be beneficial to both this student and his or her student mentor?		
Can this student chart progress to take more ownership and responsibility for his or her learning?		
Is this student experiencing more accomplishments than frustrations with his or her inclusion experience in your class?		
Has physical inclusion allowed this student to develop a more positive self-image, which has translated to increased self-confidence and motivation?		
Are you experiencing personal and/or professional growth by having this student in your class?		

Answer Key

STOP AND FIND NEW WORDS! (PAGE 11)

Two letters: as, pa

Three letters: ape, asp, lap, pal, pea, sap, sea, see, spa

Four letters: apes, ease, laps, leap, pale, pals, peal, peas, peel, plea, sale, seal, seep, slap

Five letters: leaps, lease, pales, peals, peels, pleas, sleep

WRITE IT, SHOW IT, KNOW IT! (PAGE 54)

Words	Decimal	Fraction	Picture
1. one-half	.5	$\frac{1}{2}$	Pictures
2. two-thirds	.66	$\frac{2}{3}$	may vary
3. six-eighths	.75	$\frac{6}{8}$	
4. five-fifths	1	$\frac{5}{5}$ or 1	
5. two and two-thirds	2.66	$2\frac{2}{3}$	

	Less Than 1 Whole	1 Whole	More Than 1 Whole
1.	X		
2.	X		
3.	X		
4.		X	
5.			X

READ THE SIGNS (PAGE 55)

1. A		**2.** B
3. B		**4.** A
5. A		**6.** B
7. A		**8.** A

TRICKY TOOTHPICKS (PAGE 58)

1. Move 2 toothpicks to make 7 squares.

2. Move 4 toothpicks to make 10 squares.

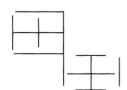

3. Remove 2 toothpicks to make 2 squares.

4. Move 3 toothpicks to make 3 squares.

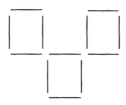

TECHNO TANGRAMS (PAGE 59)

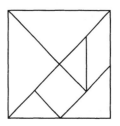

MATTER AND YOU (PAGE 66)

1. P		**2.** C
3. C		**4.** P
5. C		**6.** P
7. P		**8.** C
9. C		**10.** P

AMAZING MNEMONICS (PAGE 70)

1. Order of eight planets from the sun: Mercury, Venus, Earth, Mars, Jupiter, Saturn, Uranus, Neptune

2. Five Great Lakes: Huron, Ontario, Michigan, Erie, Superior

3. Notes on a musical scale: E, G, B, D, F

4. Seven continents: S. America, Europe, Asia, N. America, Australia, Antarctica, Africa

5. Order of operations in solving equations: Parentheses, Exponents, Multiplication, Division, Addition, Subtraction

6. Colors in a rainbow: Red, Orange, Yellow, Green, Blue, Indigo, Violet

UNDERSTANDING DIFFERENCES (PAGE 83)

3. Some students see things differently than you do.

References

Armbruster, B., Lehr, F., & Osborn, J. *Put reading first: The research building blocks for teaching children to read: kindergarten through grade 3.* (2001). Retrieved May 9, 2006, from the National Institute for Literacy Web site: http:// http://www.nifl.gov/partnershipforreading/publications/reading_first1.html#phonemic.

Curiouser.co.uk. *Tangram template.* Retrieved June 19, 2005, from http://www.curiouser.co.uk/tangram/template.htm.

Fairfax County, Virginia. *Booklists for elementary age children.* Retrieved May 20, 2006, from http://www.fairfaxcounty.gov/library/reading/elem/.

Harriott, W. (2004). *Inclusion inservice: Content and training procedures across the United States.* Journal of Special Education Leadership, 17, 91–102.

Hoffman, M., & Binch, C. (1991). *Amazing Grace.* New York: Dial Books.

Karten, T. J. (2005). *Inclusion strategies that work! Research-based methods for the classroom.* Thousand Oaks, CA: Corwin Press.

McTighe, H., Seif, E., & Wiggins, G. (2004). *You can teach for meaning.* Educational Leadership, 62, 26–30.

National Council for the Social Studies. (2002). *Expectations of excellence: Curriculum standards for social studies.* Silverspring, MD: National Council for the Social Studies (NCSS).

National Council of Teachers of English and International Reading Association. (1996). *Standards for the English language arts.* Urbana, IL: National Council of Teachers of English (NCTE).

National Council of Teachers of Mathematics. (2005). *Principles and standards for school mathematics.* Reston, VA: National Council of Teachers of Mathematics (NCTM).

National Research Council. (2005). *National science education standards.* Washington, DC: National Academy Press.

Nolet, V., & McLaughlin, M. (2005). *Accessing the general education curriculum: Including students with disabilities in standards-based reform.* Thousand Oaks, CA: Corwin Press.

Odom, S., Brantlinger, E., Gersten, R., Horner, R., Thompson, B., & Harris, K. (2005). *Research in special education: Scientific methods and evidence-based practices.* Exceptional Children, 71, 137–148.

Walsh, J., & Conner, T. (2004). *Increasing participation by students with disabilities in standards-based reform through teacher observations.* Journal of Special Education Leadership, 17, 103–110.

Yell, M., Katsiyanna, A., & Shiner, J. (2006). *Improving student services: The no child left behind act, adequate yearly progress, and students with disabilities.* Teaching Exceptional Children, 38, 32–39.

Young, S. (1994). *Scholastic rhyming dictionary.* New York: Scholastic Inc.

Zull, J. (2004). *The art of changing the brain.* Educational Leadership, 62, 68–72.

Printed in the United States
By Bookmasters